WATCH OUT FOR SPROUTS!

FOR SPROUTS
(I'M NOTHING IF NOT A HYPOCRITE)

A TEMPLAR BOOK
FIRST PUBLISHED IN THE UK
IN 2005 BY TEMPLAR PUBLISHING
AN IMPRINT OF THE TEMPLAR COMPANY PLC
PIPPBROOK MILL, LONDON ROAD, DORKING, SURREY, RH4 1JE, UK
WWW.TEMPLARCO.CO.UK

THE ART IN THIS BOOK WAS RENDERED IN
PENCIL & PAINT WHILST SUFFERING FROM A SWOLLEN FOOT!

DESIGNED BY MIKE JOLLEY
EDITED BY A.J. WOOD
MADE IN ENGLAND
BIG THANKS TO NICOLA AND ALISON

WATCH OUT FOR SPROUTS!

POEMS, PICTURES,
DOODLES AND SERIOUS
BRAIN-THINKING BY
SIMON BARTRAM

templar publishing

THE CONTENTS OF MY BRAIN
AND THIS BOOK!

DON'T WORRY
HANDS USED FOR TICKLIN' ONLY
BE GONE POETS!
HANDS OFF
WORDSWORTH
KEEP AWAY
BYRON
YOU WRITE
YOUR OWN POEMS
'CAUSE THIS ONE'S
MY ONE!
NDERLAND
AMPIONS
2005

WHAT HAPPENED TO THE PIRATE'S EYE?

WHAT HAPPENED TO THE PIRATE'S EYE?
TELL ME WHY IS HE WEARING THAT PATCH?
IS ONE EYE BLUE AND THE OTHER EYE GREEN
AND HE'S EMBARRASSED THAT THEY DON'T MATCH?

WHAT HAPPENED TO THE PIRATE'S EYE?
WAS IT PLUCKED OUT IN A BATTLE?
PERHAPS HIS GLASS ONE DOESN'T QUITE FIT
SO WHEN HE NODS HIS HEAD IT RATTLES

WHAT HAPPENED TO THE PIRATE'S EYE?
IT COULD WELL HAVE A NERVOUS TICK
AND BE A-WINKIN' AND A-BLINKIN'
A CONDITION HE JUST CAN'T LICK

WHAT HAPPENED TO THE PIRATE'S EYE?
HAS IT GOT CONJUNCTIVITIS?
HE'D BE QUITE CONTAGIOUS SO KEEP AWAY
IS WHAT I'D WARN THE OTHER PIRATES

EYE-DROPS

WHAT HAPPENED TO THE PIRATE'S EYE?
PERHAPS HIS PARROT PECKED IT OUT
AND GOBBLED IT DOWN WITH PARSNIPS AND PEAS
AND A GENEROUS PORTION OF SPROUTS

WHAT HAPPENED TO THE PIRATE'S EYE?
HE COULD HAVE USED IT AS A BALL
FOR A GAME OF GOLF OR TENNIS OR SQUASH
OR JUST TO BOUNCE AGAINST THE WALL

PATCH
FOR THE
MATCH

MAYBE THE PIRATE'S EYE IS FINE
AND HE WEARS THE PATCH FOR FASHION
HE'S ALWAYS LOVED HIS HAUTE COUTURE
AND FOR HATS HE HAS A PASSION!

SO LIKE A CURIOUS CAT I ASKED HIM
"WHAT'S THAT PATCH ABOUT?" I SAID
"THAT'S PERSONAL!" HE ANSWERED
HIS FACE WENT BEETROOT RED

PARTY
PATCH

I DIDN'T DARE TO ASK AGAIN
I PUT THE SUBJECT FROM MY HEAD
SO MY BRAIN WAS FREE TO WONDER
ABOUT HIS WOODEN LEG INSTEAD!

DUKE BOX

DUKE BOX WAS A SINGER
PERFORMING EVERY DAY
HE STOOD STILL IN THE CORNER
CROONING FOR HIS PAY

YOU'D GET ONE SONG FOR 20P
FOR 50 YOU'D GET THREE
BUT KICK HIM ON HIS LEFT-HAND SIDE
AND YOU'D GET THEM ALL FOR FREE

14

NEW OLD MACDONALD

OLD MACDONALD HAD A FARM
EE-1-EE-1-O
BUT HE HATED THE EARLY MORNINGS
SO HE MADE HIS COWS
INTO BURGERS

MOO!

AND HE OPENED UP FAST FOOD JOINTS
ALL OVER THE WORLD
AND HE SOLD ALL THE BURGERS
IN ALL THE FAST FOOD JOINTS
ALL OVER THE WORLD
AND HE NEVER LOOKED BACK!
EE-1-EE-1-O

THE DOG ATE MY HOMEWORK

I WOULDN'T DREAM OF EATING ANYONE'S HOMEWORK. I HAVE THE UTMOST RESPECT FOR KNOWLEDGE AND LEARNING AND ANYWAY I WAS OUT ALL NIGHT CHASIN' CATS WITH ROVER AND THAT NEW CHAP WHO CALLS HIMSELF FITZGIBBON CRUMBLE. GO AND ASK THEM. IT'S NO WORD OF A LIE GUV'NOR!

SIR I'M VERY SORRY TO TELL YOU
AND I'LL LOOK YOU STRAIGHT IN THE EYE
BUT LAST NIGHT THE DOG ATE MY HOMEWORK
AND I SWEAR THAT'S NO WORD OF A LIE

WELL PERHAPS THAT'S NOT QUITE THE WHOLE TRUTH
THERE'S A LITTLE BIT MORE I SHOULD TELL
SEE, THE DOG ONLY ATE UP MY GERMAN
BUT MY FAMILY WAS HUNGRY AS WELL

MY MOTHER MUNCHED DOWN ALL THE ENGLISH
WITH A MIXTURE OF MEXICAN DIPS
AND THEN DAD DEVOURED THE GEOGRAPHY
WITH MUSHROOMS, BEANS AND CHIPS

MY GRAN BOILED UP ALL THE CHEMISTRY
IT WENT THICK AND GOOEY AND BLUE
BUT GRANDAD GULPED IT ALL STRAIGHT DOWN
IN A DISH CALLED CHEMISTRY STEW

MY BROTHER THEN CHEWED ON A FILLET OF MATHS
BUT HE SPAT IT RIGHT BACK OUT
AND IT LEFT A MOST HORRIBLE AFTERTASTE
AND GUNGE ON THE ROOF OF HIS MOUTH

MY UNCLE SAVOURED MY BEAUTIFUL ART
"A FEAST FOR THE SENSES" HE RECKONED
SO I PICKED UP MY PENCILS, MY PAPER AND PAINTS
AND SAT RIGHT DOWN TO DRAW HIM SOME SECONDS

THEN MY AUNTY THREW UP IN THE TOILET
IT WAS THAT HISTORY CURRY I THINK
ITS 'BEST BEFORE' DATE SHOWED THAT HISTORY WAS OLD
AND IN TRUTH IT WAS STARTING TO STINK!

SO AGAIN SIR I'M HONESTLY SORRY TO SAY
I CAN'T HAND IN MY HOMEWORK ON TIME
BUT MY DAD WROTE A LONG AND EXPLANATORY NOTE
TO CONFIRM IT'S NOT REALLY MY CRIME

BUT ALAS SIR THIS MORNING MY BREAKFAST I MISSED
AND ON THE BUS AS I TRAVELLED TO SCHOOL
MY TUMMY WITH HUNGER DID RUMBLE AND MOAN
AND MY CHOPS BEGAN DRIPPING WITH DROOL

I HAD NOTHING TO EAT IN MY SCHOOL BAG
NOT A MORSEL OF CHEESE IN MY COAT
AND I JUST COULDN'T WAIT 'TIL THAT DINNERTIME BELL
SO I ATE DAD'S EXPLANATORY NOTE!

A MESSAGE FOR BOYS

BEWARE OF MONSTERS
WITH BIG SHARP TEETH
OF ROCKS IN THE DESERT
WITH SCORPIONS BENEATH

BEWARE OF SHARKS
WITH COLD BLACK EYES
OF STARCHED WHITE SHIRTS
WITH BORING TIES

WATCH OUT FOR SPROUTS
THE COLOUR OF SNOT
MAM SAYS THAT THEY'RE NICE
BUT YOU KNOW THAT THEY'RE NOT

DON'T TRUST ANY TEACHER
NOT A SIR OR A MISS
OR PINK-LIPSTICKED GRANNIES
WHO BEG FOR A KISS

BEWARE OF BATHTIME
OF SWEET-SMELLING SOAP —
A BOY WITHOUT MUCK
IS A BOY WITHOUT HOPE

BUT THE SCARIEST THINGS
OF WHICH BOYS MUST BEWARE
ARE THOSE THINGS THEY CALL GIRLS
LIKE THAT ONE OVER THERE

SHE LOOKS PRETTY AND SWEET
WITH HER LIPS ROSY RED
BUT IF GIVEN A CHANCE
SHE'D BITE OFF YOUR HEAD

WITH A BOTTLE OF POP
SHE'D WASH IT RIGHT DOWN
THEN WAIT FOR THE NEXT BOY
TO COME INTO TOWN

I WON'T LET HER GET ME
I'LL PELT HER WITH PEAS
THEN RUN QUICKLY PAST
WHEN SHE'S DOWN ON HER KNEES

I'LL SHOOT DOWN THE ROAD
ROUND ITS CORNERS AND CURLS
YES, THAT'S WHAT TO DO
WHEN YOU RUN INTO GIRLS

SEE?

DAD

MY DAD IS ANCIENT

HE WAS BORN IN THE OLDEN DAYS IN 1968
I THINK HE WAS BORN IN A CAVE
A CAVE WITH NO TELLY
AND HE WAS HAIRY
IN FACT EVERYONE WAS HAIRY IN 1968
(I'VE SEEN THE RECORD COVERS)

AND I'M ALMOST CERTAIN THERE WERE NO CARS
OR CHOCOLATE OR PROPER TOYS LIKE COMPUTER GAMES
OR THOSE FIGURES YOU GET FREE WITH BURGERS
DAD ONLY HAD A STONE FOOTBALL AND SOME STRING
BUT HE DID SHARE A BIKE WITH UNCLE FRED
ALTHOUGH I THINK IT HAD
SQUARE WHEELS

UG!

I'LL BET IT WOULD HAVE BEEN VERY EASY
TO CRASH INTO LAMPPOSTS
ON A BIKE WITH SQUARE WHEELS
THEN AGAIN THERE WERE NO LAMPPOSTS IN 1968
SO THAT WAS OK

ANYWAY DAD ALWAYS SAYS
HE PREFERRED PLAYING WITH THE CAT
IT WASN'T LIKE CATS TODAY THOUGH! OH NO!
IT HAD BIGGER TEETH AND STRANGE FUR LIKE A TIGER!
AND IT DIDN'T MIAOW. IT ROARED!!
LIKE A GIGANTIC TERRIFYING

BEAST!

AND THEY CALLED IT POPSY

OH! AND SUPERMARKETS WEREN'T OPEN 24 HOURS LIKE THEY ARE TODAY
SO PEOPLE HAD TO HUNT FOR FOOD

IN TRIBES!

UNCLE FRED, GRANDAD AND BIG AUNTY BRENDA WERE IN MY DAD'S TRIBE
POPSY WOULD GO ALONG TOO SOMETIMES
AND THEY MAINLY LIKED TO CATCH

DINOSAURS

I THINK!

DAD SAYS DINOSAURS TASTED BEST
WITH SPAGHETTI HOOPS
HMMM, LOVELY!
BUT REMEMBER!! THERE WAS NO KETCHUP IN THOSE DAYS
JUST BROWN SAUCE

THERE'S MORE...

AND DAD WAS SO BUSY HUNTING
THAT HE ONLY WENT TO SCHOOL ONCE A WEEK!
IT WAS MILES AND MILES AND MILES AWAY
AND THE BUSES WEREN'T REGULAR
SO HE HAD TO WALK THERE
WITHOUT PROPER TRAINERS
OVER DESERTS AND GLACIERS
AND IT TOOK MORE THAN AN HOUR!
IT WAS A HARD LIFE

AND SCHOOL WAS VERY DIFFERENT
KIDS DIDN'T LEARN ALGEBRA AND FRACTIONS
NO, INSTEAD THEY LEARNED HOW TO WRESTLE CROCODILES
AND BUILD HUTS OUT OF TREE BRANCHES

IN A WAY

I DON'T THINK PEOPLE WERE QUITE AS BRAINY IN 1968
MOST OF THE TIME THEY JUST SHOUTED AND POINTED
AND SAID THINGS LIKE "UG, UG" TO EACH OTHER

THINKING ABOUT IT DAD HAS DONE VERY WELL
BECOMING A CROWN COURT JUDGE AND ALL THAT
CONSIDERING HIS CHILDHOOD

I THINK MAM MUST HAVE HELPED HIM A LOT
IT WAS DIFFERENT FOR HER
SHE WAS BORN IN A PRIVATE HOSPITAL IN BIRMINGHAM IN 1977
AND GREW UP IN A FOUR-BEDROOM SEMI JUST OUTSIDE SUTTON COLDFIELD
SHE HAD A NORMAL CAT,
TWO TELLIES (ONE COLOUR)
AND SHE WENT TO A SCHOOL WHERE SHE HAD TO WEAR A STRAW HAT
AND PLAY HOCKEY

SHE ALWAYS JOKES THAT DAD IS THE POOR RELATION
AS WELL AS BEING ANCIENT
LIFE WAS HARDER...
IN 1968

DAD NOW

SNEEZE

TODAY A SPIDER CRAWLED RIGHT UP MY NOSE
TO SHELTER FROM THE RAIN
'THOUGH FINE BY ME
SO TICKLY WAS HE
THAT I SNEEZED HIM RIGHT OUT AGAIN!

SKIN

I QUITE LIKE MY SKIN
IT HOLDS ALL OF ME IN
CAUSING MINIMUM FUSS
WHICH IS ALWAYS A PLUS

IF I DIDN'T HAVE SKIN
TO HOLD ALL OF ME IN
MY POOR GUTS WOULD BE FOUND
STREWN ALL OVER THE GROUND

FUTURE

HERE COMES THE FUTURE
WE'LL MEET IT NOW AT LAST
THREE, TWO, ONE
HELLO, GOODBYE
THAT FUTURE'S NOW THE PAST

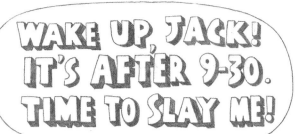

JACK
THE LAZY
GIANT-KILLER

JACK THE LAZY GIANT-KILLER
WAS AS DOCILE AS A SLOTH
JUST TO GET OUT OF BED
AND STEP ON AN ANT
TO HIM
WAS TAXING ENOUGH

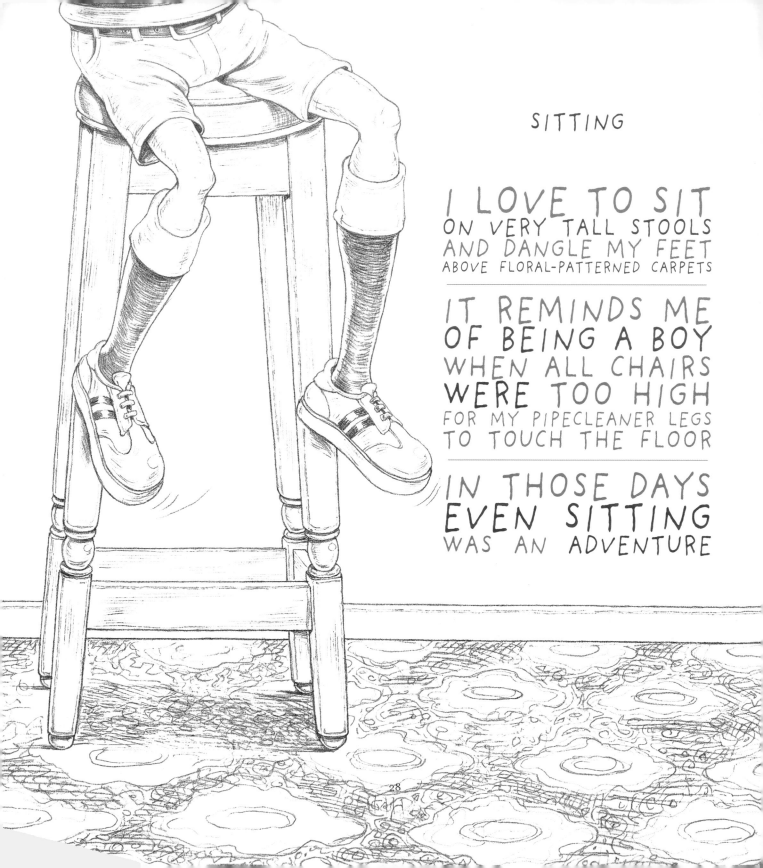

SITTING

I LOVE TO SIT
ON VERY TALL STOOLS
AND DANGLE MY FEET
ABOVE FLORAL-PATTERNED CARPETS

IT REMINDS ME
OF BEING A BOY
WHEN ALL CHAIRS
WERE TOO HIGH
FOR MY PIPECLEANER LEGS
TO TOUCH THE FLOOR

IN THOSE DAYS
EVEN SITTING
WAS AN ADVENTURE

SUNDAY

I WISH IT WASN'T SUNDAY
I DON'T LIKE GRANDAD'S SNORING
I HATE THE TASTE OF CARROTS AND SPROUTS
AND STATELY HOMES ARE BORING

I WISH IT WASN'T SUNDAY
I HAVE TO DRESS UP TIDY AND SMART
AND MY MAM TELLS ME OFF WHEN WE'RE SITTING IN CHURCH
IF I BURP OR FIDGET OR FART

I WISH IT WASN'T SUNDAY
MY MATE BILLY IS NEVER AROUND
SO THERE'S NO PLAYING FOOTBALL OR SEARCHING FOR FROGS
AND NO RACING OUR BIKES AROUND TOWN

I WISH IT WASN'T SUNDAY
I'M SO BORED I'VE A PERMANENT YAWN
AND IT'S AWFULLY UNFAIR THAT MY DAD HAS A NAP
JUST AS I HAVE TO MOW THE BACK LAWN

I WISH IT WASN'T SUNDAY
I'VE ALWAYS GOT HOMEWORK TO DO
AND BY THE TIME THAT I'VE FINISHED IT'S BATHTIME THEN BED
AS THE STARS JUST BEGIN TO PEEK THROUGH

AND THEN ONE DAY ON AND IT'S NOW TIME FOR SCHOOL
AND IT'S MATHS FIRST THING ON A MONDAY
WHAT A TERRIBLE WAY TO BEGIN THE LONG WEEK
OH I REALLY DO WISH IT WAS SUNDAY!!

IDENTICAL TWIN
IDENTICAL TWIN

MY IDENTICAL TWIN IS CALLED TOM
AND HIS EYES ARE EXACTLY LIKE MINE
WE HAVE GLISTENING WHITE TEETH
WITH BIG CHINS UNDERNEATH
AND FOLK THINK THAT HE'S ME
ALL THE TIME

WE'RE JUST LIKE TWO PEAS IN A POD
YOU ALMOST COULD SWEAR WE WERE CLONES
IF YOU HAD X-RAY EYES
IT WOULD BE NO SURPRISE
THAT WE'RE SIMILAR RIGHT DOWN
TO OUR BONES

OUR EARS COULDN'T BE MORE ALIKE
WE SHARE THE SAME PLATES-OF-MEAT FEET
HIS DUPLICATE NOSE
ECHOES MINE WHEN IT BLOWS
AND WE BOTH TURN BRIGHT PINK
IN THE HEAT

SO THEN HOW CAN YOU TELL US APART
OR SPOT WHEN WE SWOP OR WE SWITC
AT THE END OF THE DAY
THERE'S JUST ONE EASY WAY
FOR YOU TO BE SURE WHICH
ONE'S WHICH

WE'VE ONE HUNDRED AND TWO FRECKLES EACH
WE BLUSH BRIGHTLY AT ALL THE WRONG TIMES
THERE'S ONE HISTORY ATTACHED
TO OUR BIRTHMARKS THAT MATCH
ON OUR BITS WHERE THE SUN
DOESN'T SHINE

YOU SEE WE'RE BOTH RAVING
FOOTBALL FANATICS
I'M A RED AND WHITE SUNDERLAND FAN
BUT TOM'S LOST HIS HEAD
HE'S BEEN TOO EASILY LED
AND HE'S A BLACK AND WHITE
NEWCASTLE MAN

OVERGROWN POEM

MY NEXT-DOOR NEIGHBOUR NEVER CUTS HIS GRASS
HIS LAWN IS LIKE A BIG GREEN BEARD
CRUSTED WITH LAST NIGHT'S DINNER
I COULDN'T TELL YOU WHY HE DOESN'T MOW IT
BUT IF HE DID IT WOULD REVEAL THE FORGOTTEN DOG-EARED SECRETS

OF DAYS GONE BY

THERE WE WOULD FIND
ONE WHEELBARROW WITH NO WHEEL
ONE GENTLEMAN'S TOP-HAT
ONE FOOTBALL THAT LITTLE BILLY MCCALL SLICED OVER THE FENCE
WHEN RECREATING THE WINNING GOAL OF THE 1973 CUP FINAL (BILLY'S THIRTY-SIX NOW)

WE'D DISCOVER

TWO POLYSTYRENE CHIP CARTONS CAKED IN SOLIDIFIED GRAVY
FROM THAT CHIPPY THAT IS NOW A HEALTH FOOD SHOP

WE'D FIND

FIVE GOLD RINGS (CHEAP)

TWO SHOES—SAME STYLE, DIFFERENT SIZES (ODD!)

FOUR DELICATE SKELETONS OF MICE THAT JUGGLING CATS HAVE LONG SINCE STOPPED TOYING WITH AND ONE DOLLY BELONGING TO A BABY GIRL WHO IS NOW GROWN AND HAS A BABY GIRL OF HER OWN

AND WE'D SPY SEVEN DISORIENTED ALIENS

302 WORMS YET TO SEE THE LIGHT OF DAY AND ONE SOGGY NEWSPAPER OPEN AT THE T.V. SECTION REVIEWING SITCOMS AND PLAYS THAT NO-ONE REMEMBERS

AND MAYBE, FINALLY,

IN THE DEEPEST, DARKEST, GLOOMIEST CORNER OF THAT SORRY GARDEN WHERE THE GRASS SWISHES IN THE WIND AND STANDS AS TALL AS THE HOUSE

WE WOULD FIND, SITTING
NEGLECTED AND SAD,
THE LONELY FRAME

OF AN OLD, DENTED AND RUSTY... LAWNMOWER!

PUDDLE TROUBLE

CAN YOU HEAR MY MAM? SHE'S HOWLING AT ME
HER FACE IS AS RED AS RED CAN BE
"YOU BETTER NOT JUMP IN THAT THERE PUDDLE
OR MARK MY WORDS THERE'LL BE BIG TROUBLE"

NOW I'M NOT QUITE SURE WHAT TROUBLE SHE MEANS
IT LOOKS JUST LIKE MOST PUDDLES I'VE SEEN
BUT PERHAPS THIS ONE HAS HIDDEN FLAWS
AND IS FULL TO THE BRIM WITH DINOSAURS

OR MAYBE THERE'S SHARKS OR PIRANHA-TYPE FISH
WHO'D CONSIDER MY TOES A DELECTABLE DISH
OR THE GHOST OF DEAD PIRATES WHO LONG AGO DROWNED
WHEN SEARCHING FOR TREASURE IN SHIPWRECKS DEEP DOWN

ARE THE WATERS TOO CHOPPY, THE CURRENTS TOO WILD?
COULD THEY SHAKE OR UNBALANCE A DELICATE CHILD?
ARE THERE NUCLEAR BOMBS FIRED BY SMALL SUBMARINES
FIGHTING SAD PUDDLE WARS THAT OUR WORLD HASN'T SEEN

AND A JUMP WITH BOTH FEET WILL NO DOUBT END IN FAILURE
IF THE PUDDLE'S SO DEEP I SINK DOWN TO AUSTRALIA
OR A GIANT PINK SQUID TAKES A FANCY TO ME
AND HUGS ME SO TIGHT THAT I CANNOT BREAK FREE

OR MAYBE IT'S CRAMMED FULL OF RUBBISH AND STUFF
AND TO FIND ROOM FOR ME WOULD PROVE REALLY QUITE TOUGH
WELL, IT'S DRIVING ME MAD, I JUST HAVE TO FIND OUT
WHAT THAT PUDDLE'S DARK SECRET COULD BE ALL ABOUT!

WHILE MY MAM ISN'T LOOKING TOWARDS IT I'LL DASH
I'M READY TO JUMP! HERE GOES! 1-2-3 SPLASH
NOW I'M IN IT AND WAITING FOR TROUBLE TO COME
BUT THERE'S NO BIG KERFUFFLE, NO SMALL SNIFF OF FUN

NO SHARKS, NO PIRANHAS, NO SAD PUDDLE WARS
NO PIRATES, NO BOMBS AND NO SQUID HUGS OF COURSE
TO BE HONEST THIS PUDDLE IS JUST VERY WET
IN FACT IT'S AS WET AS A PUDDLE CAN GET

AND THE TROUBLE WITH JUMPING IN PUDDLES LIKE THAT
IS THAT WHEN I GET CAUGHT BY MY MAM OR MY DAD
I'LL GET CLIPPED ROUND THE EAR'OLE– IT'S REALLY BAD NEWS
AND GET SENT TO BED EARLY FOR RUINING MY SHOES!

(AND WHAT MAKES IT WORSE, IF I MAY BE SO BOLD, IS THAT THIS YEAR I'LL BE 37 YEARS OLD!)

THE BATTERED SAUSAGE

BIFF, BANG, BOFF
THE SAUSAGE WAS TIRED OF BEING
BATTERED
SO EACH DAY HE WENT TO THE GYM
HE TOOK BOXING LESSONS
AND LIFTED THE HEAVIEST DUMBBELLS
MONTHS LATER HE EMERGED
TRANSFORMED INTO
A JUMBO
SAUSAGE!
AND JUMBO SAUSAGES AREN'T USUALLY
BATTERED
(AT LEAST NOT IN MY LOCAL CHIP SHOP)

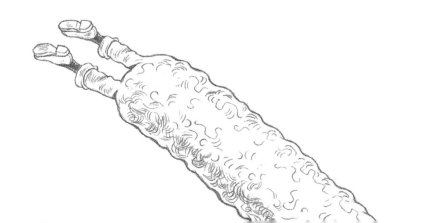

SAUSAGES

IF SAUSAGES HAD LEGS
THEY'D RUN AND RUN AND RUN
THEY'D HURDLE AND THEY'D LEAP
AND FROLIC IN THE SUN

IF SAUSAGES HAD LEGS
THEY'D WIGGLE, JIG AND DANCE
THEY'D SPLOSH AND SPLASH IN RIVERS
AND WEAR EXCITING PANTS

IF SAUSAGES HAD LEGS
THEY'D CROSS THE WORLD ON STILTS
THEY'D RIDE ELEPHANTS IN INDIA
IN SCOTLAND THEY'D WEAR KILTS

IF SAUSAGES HAD LEGS
THEY'D RULE THE EARTH IN TIME
THEY'D PASS STRICT SAUSAGE LAWS
TO KEEP US ALL IN LINE

IF SAUSAGES HAD LEGS
THEY'D VENTURE INTO SPACE
THEY'D HOP AROUND THE PLANETS
AND ADVANCE THE SAUSAGE RACE

BUT SAUSAGES DON'T HAVE LEGS
THEY CAN'T DANCE OR WIGGLE THEIR HIPS
THEY JUST SIT RIGHT HERE, UPON MY PLATE
WITH MUSHROOMS, BEANS AND CHIPS

I THINK I'M IN THE WRONG BOOK. IS THIS CHAPTER SEVEN OF 'WOOL FASHION FOR THE MODERN ROBOT'? IF NOT I'M IN DEEP TROUBLE. BE SURE OF IT.

KNOW YOUR

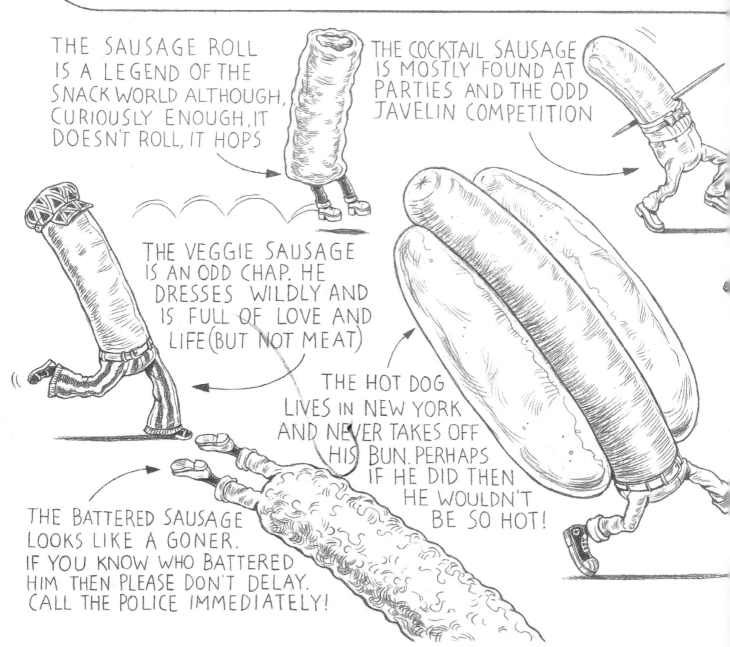

THE SAUSAGE ROLL IS A LEGEND OF THE SNACK WORLD ALTHOUGH, CURIOUSLY ENOUGH, IT DOESN'T ROLL, IT HOPS

THE COCKTAIL SAUSAGE IS MOSTLY FOUND AT PARTIES AND THE ODD JAVELIN COMPETITION

THE VEGGIE SAUSAGE IS AN ODD CHAP. HE DRESSES WILDLY AND IS FULL OF LOVE AND LIFE (BUT NOT MEAT)

THE HOT DOG LIVES IN NEW YORK AND NEVER TAKES OFF HIS BUN. PERHAPS IF HE DID THEN HE WOULDN'T BE SO HOT!

THE BATTERED SAUSAGE LOOKS LIKE A GONER. IF YOU KNOW WHO BATTERED HIM THEN PLEASE DON'T DELAY. CALL THE POLICE IMMEDIATELY!

SAUSAGES

...NOT BE 100% ACCURATE

LINKS OF SAUSAGE MAINLY CONSIST OF SAD SAUSAGES WHO DON'T LIKE BEING ALONE

THE SPICY SAUSAGE IS BOTH MYSTERIOUS AND EXOTIC. HE HAILS FROM FAR-AWAY LANDS AND LEARNED TO SPEAK GOOD ENGLISH BY WATCHING OLD BLACK & WHITE FILMS SET IN SURREY

THE CUMBERLAND IS THE ONLY KNOWN SAUSAGE NOT TO HAVE LEGS AND LAY UNDISCOVERED UNTIL THE YEAR 1973

THE JUMBO SAUSAGE LOOKS MEAN BUT HAS A HEART OF GOLD. HE WEARS XXXL TROUSERS AND SIZE FIFTEEN BOBBA BOOTS

CHIPOLATAS ARE SMALL BUT PERFECTLY FORMED. THEY LOVE CHRISTMAS

MORE SAUSAGE INFORMATION ABOUT SAUSAGES WILL BE AVAILABLE ON THE 3RD AUGUST 2016 - MAYBE!

APPOPOLLIS THE ANCIENT GREEK

APPOPOLLIS WAS AN ANCIENT GREEK
BUT NOT THAT KIND FROM HISTORY
HE KNEW NOWT ABOUT PHILOSOPHY
HIS LIFE WAS NOT A MYSTERY
YOU SEE
HE OWNED THE KEBAB SHOP TWO DOORS DOWN
DID APPOPOLLIS THE GREEK
AND HE REALLY WAS QUITE ANCIENT
NINETY-TWO WHEN HE CROAKED LAST WEEK

BEAUTIFUL ON THE INSIDE

YOU'RE BEAUTIFUL ON THE INSIDE
YOUR SPLEEN IS A BIT OF A CUTEY
YOUR LIVER'S SO HANDSOME, YOUR KIDNEY'S QUITE DISHY
YOUR INTESTINES ARE RADIANT WITH BEAUTY

YOUR SKELETON IS CATWALK MATERIAL
YOUR HEART SHINES AS BRIGHT AS THE SUN
YES, YOU'RE BEAUTIFUL ON THE INSIDE
'THOUGH YOUR FACE DOES RESEMBLE YOUR BUM!

IF YOUR GUTS
WERE A PLACE
THEY WOULD BE
THIS PLACE

IF YOUR FACE
WAS A PLACE
IT WOULD BE
THIS PLACE

DUCK CHALLENGED ROOSTER...

'NO WAY!'

SAID ROOSTER

'CHICKEN!'

SAID DUCK

DO I KNOW YOU?

(A SAD TALE OF LONELINESS AND REJECTION)

DO I KNOW YOU?
I'M SURE I RECOGNISE YOU
YOU'RE QUITE SMALL, AREN'T YOU?
AND SORT OF ROUNDISH
HAVEN'T I SEEN YOU
AT THE GOLF CLUB?

CHEER UP!
YOU'RE A BIT OF A MISERY TO BE HONEST
WHAT'S THAT YOU SAY?
PEOPLE IGNORE YOU AT SUNDAY LUNCH?
THEY MOAN AT THE SIGHT OF YOU?

HMM... I SUPPOSE YOU ARE A
LITTLE STRANGE AND GREEN
A BIT LEAFY TOO!
ARE YOU SURE I DON'T KNOW YOU?
COME ON NOW, CHEER UP!
WHAT DID YOU SAY?

DID YOU SAY "EVEN THE MOST RAVENOUS OF
HUNGRY MAD GIANTS
WOULD SPIT YOU OUT?"
I DON'T KNOW WHAT YOU'RE TALKING ABOUT

I'M SURE I...
WAIT A MINUTE
YOU'RE NOT, ARE YOU?
SAY YOU'RE NOT...
PLEASE! OH NO!
YOU REALLY ARE
IT'S TRUE!
YOU'RE... A... A...
YOU'RE A
SPROUT!
AAARRRGGGHHHHH!!!!

GET AWAY FROM ME
I HATE YOU
AAARRRGGGHHHHH!!!!
AND STAY AWAY!
(AND THE LONELY OLD SPROUT SLOWLY ROLLED AWAY SIGHING
AND WISHING THINGS COULD HAVE BEEN DIFFERENT)

NINE REASONS TO AVOID SPROUTS

1 THEY WEAR BAD HATS

2 THEY'RE THE MOST TERRIBLE DANCERS

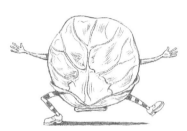

3 THEY SUPPORT YOU-KNOW-WHO!

4 THEY'RE EITHER SWOTS....

5 ....OR GOOD-FOR-NOTHING LAZY WASTERS

6 THEY'VE NEVER HEARD OF DEODORANT

7 THEY'RE SHOW OFFS

8 THEY'RE ARGUMENTATIVE

NO WE'RE NOT!

9 THEY AREN'T MADE OF CHOCOLATE

IS THAT REALLY MY FAULT?

YES

ALL POINTS ALSO APPLY TO BROCCOLI (APART FROM 2,3,4,5,6,7+9)

LIFE?

LIFE ON **OTHER** PLANETS
I'M SURE WE'LL **NEVER** SEE
THE **VERY IDEA**, I'LL HONESTLY SAY,
IS **ALIEN** TO ME.

THE ICEMAN GOETH

IF I **DIE TODAY** I DON'T WANT A WAKE
A **KNEES-UP INSTEAD** WOULD BE **NICE**
BUT **SCIENTISTS** PLAN
TO **CRYOGENICALLY FREEZE ME**
SO YOU'D **BEST PUT** THE **PARTY** ON **ICE**

DOOM AND GLOOM

BARRY **DOOM** AND GAVIN **GLOOM**
SAT *INSIDE* THEIR **MURKY ROOM**
PONDERING **IMPENDING DOOM**
UNTIL **SURE ENOUGH** THE WORLD WENT...

IT WILL BE A SHAME THE DAY THE WORLD ENDS

IT WILL BE A SHAME THE DAY THE WORLD ENDS
WHEN THE SPINNING GRINDS DOWN TO A STOP
TOO LATE THEN TO FINISH ALL THE THINGS WE'VE BEGUN
AS TIME ENDS WITH A BANG AND A POP

IF OUR GLOBE IS GULPED DOWN BY A HUNGRY SPACE TROLL
IF IT CRUMBLES OR MELTS OR JUST BREAKS
NO MECHANIC WILL FIX IT, NO STICKY-TAPE STICK IT
NO MELODY WILL SOOTH ALL ITS ACHES

TOO LATE FOR THE BOFFINS TO FINALLY DISCOVER
THE SECRETS OF EVERLASTING LIFE
NO TIME FOR YOUNG BOYS TO GROW UP AND SPROUT BEARDS
TO TASTE ALE OR TO MARRY A WIFE

AND A MILLION STRAY PIECES OF UNFINISHED JIGSAWS
FOREVER WILL END UP ALONE
AS ASTRONAUTS TEARFULLY ROAM AROUND SPACE
THEIR NEXT MISSION TO FIND A NEW HOME

NO ONE WILL KNOW HOW THE BOOK IS TO END
IF OUR HERO WILL MAKE HIS ESCAPE
OR WHAT TWIST WILL UNFOLD AT THE END OF THE FILM
WILL THEY SHOOT DOWN THAT FORTY-FOOT APE?

NO TIME IN THE GAME FOR THE GREAT WINNING GOAL
AS THE WHISTLE IS BLOWN BY THE REF
AND THE RIVERS WON'T FINISH THEIR RACE TO THE SEA
BEFORE THE WIND EXHALES HIS LAST BREATH

FINAL WORDS WILL BE WRITTEN INTO DOG-EARED DIARIES
AS WE UNPLUG OUR CITIES AND TOWNS
WE'LL TURN OFF THE SUN, DRAW THE CURTAINS OF CLOUD
AND LAST, TURN THE VOLUME RIGHT DOWN

BUT THEN WHERE WILL WE LAY OUR POOR WORLD DOWN TO REST?
ARE THERE SCRAPYARDS FOR PLANETS IN SPACE?
WILL A BIG OILY TRUCK COME TO TOW IT AWAY
AND LEAVE A NEW WORLD IN ITS PLACE

IT COULD ALL END FIVE BILLION LONG CENTURIES FROM NOW
OR TOMORROW AT A QUARTER TO THREE
I'LL NOT TAKE ANY CHANCES, NOT WASTE ANY TIME
I'LL BE THE BEST I CAN POSSIBLY BE

I'LL NOT LAZE AROUND PONDERING THE THINGS THAT COULD HAPPEN
I'LL GET UP AND GET MYSELF GOING
THERE ARE SUCH SIGHTS TO SEE, SO MUCH LEFT TO DO
AND I'LL START HERE BY FINISHING THIS POEM

YES IT WILL BE A SHAME
THE DAY OUR FANTASTIC WORLD ENDS
WHEN THE HANDS COME TO REST ON THE CLOCK
BUT I CAN'T TALK ANY LONGER, I'VE MOUNTAINS TO CLIMB
TICK TOCK, TICK TOCK, TICK TOCK

WEREWOLVES AND HIPPIES

BEWARE OF CONFUSING WEREWOLVES AND HIPPIES
THEY'RE SIMILAR IN MORE THAN ONE WAY
THEY'RE BOTH TERRIBLY HAIRY
AND OFTEN DISHEVELLED
AND LAZE AROUND MOST OF THE DAY

BUT WHILE ONE WILL HUG TREES
AND EAT COUSCOUS AND BEANS
AND PRANCE AROUND FIELDS FULL OF FLOWERS
THE OTHER WILL HAVE ONLY ONE MAIN CONCERN
AND PURSUE IT WITH ALL OF HIS POWERS

AND THAT'S
TO CHASE YOU
AND CATCH YOU
AND NIBBLE YOUR NOSE
TO SWALLOW YOUR EARS
AND CHEW ON YOUR TOES
TO BOIL BOTH YOUR EYEBALLS
AND GOBBLE THEM UP
TO GUZZLE YOUR BLOOD
FROM A NICE CHINA CUP

TO MUNCH ON YOUR FINGERS
MAKE SOUP FROM YOUR HIPS
SUCK ON YOUR BRAINS
AND THEN FRY UP YOUR LIPS
SAUTÉ YOUR TOENAILS
AND GNAW ON YOUR BONES
AND SLURP DOWN YOUR GUTS
AS YOU WIGGLE AND MOAN

SO THE POINT OF THIS POEM
ABOUT WEREWOLVES AND HIPPIES
IS TO WARN AGAINST FATAL ILLUSIONS
ONE'S WICKED, ONE'S PURE,
ONE'S CHALK AND ONE'S CHEESE
UNDERNEATH ALL THAT HAIRY CONFUSION

REMEMBER JUST THIS!
THAT HIPPIES ARE BAD
AND THEY'LL RIP YOU TO SHREDS IN A SECOND
WHEREAS WEREWOLVES ARE PEACE-LOVING
FRIENDS OF THE EARTH
I'VE GOT THAT CORRECT NOW, I RECKON

ALTHOUGH IF I'M MIXED UP, THE OMENS AREN'T GOOD
YES, I'M SURE I'LL FIND OUT PRETTY SOON
'CAUSE TONIGHT IN THE SKY
THROUGH THE STARS AND THE CLOUDS
WILL EMERGE A BRIGHT SHINING FULL MOON!

53

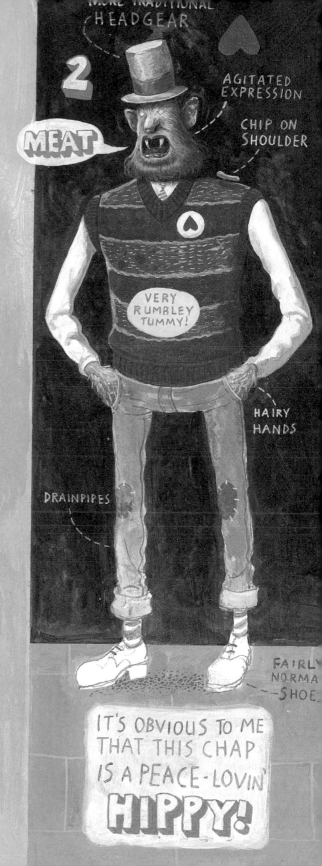

YES IT'S TRUE

NIBBLES IS A ONE TRICK PONY

BUT

IF THAT TRICK

IS TO JUGGLE SWORDS

WHILST RIDING BACKWARDS

ON A SKATEBOARD

THEN HOW MANY TRICKS

DOES A PONY

NEED?

RED INDIAN TUESDAY

TUESDAY MORNING
DEADLY RACE
BUFFALO RUN
INDIANS CHASE

PAST THE CACTUS
ACROSS THE PLAIN
OVER THE RIDGE
BACK AGAIN

CLIPPETY-CLOP
CRASH AND RUMBLE
ARROWS FLY
BUFFALO TUMBLE

THROUGH THE VALLEY
PAST THE TOWN
TOMAHAWKS SPIN
BUFFALO FROWN

MIDDAY SUN
TIME TO REST
LUNCHTIME IN
THE OLD WILD WEST

CUP OF TEA
CURRANT BUN
GAME OF TAG
HEAP GOOD FUN

ONE O'CLOCK
BACK TO THE GRIND
MUCH GOOD BUFFALO
STILL TO FIND

PAST THE CACTUS
ACROSS THE PLAIN
OVER THE RIDGE
BACK AGAIN

FIVE PAST THREE
COOLER SUN
INDIANS CHASE
BUFFALO RUN

HALF PAST FIVE
CLOCKING OFF
INDIANS LEAVE
BUFFALO STOP

PLAINS ARE STILL
STARS ARRIVE
INDIANS SLEEP
QUIET TRIBE

BUFFALO SMILE
TAKE A CHANCE
BENEATH THE MOON
THEY SING AND DANCE

I CANNOT WRITE THIS POEM
AS I HAVEN'T
A SINGLE IDEA
SO GO OFF AND AMUSE
YOURSELVES FOR A BIT
WHILE I CRANK MY BRAIN
INTO GEAR!

1

SAT ON TOILET AND WHISTLED FOR A BIT. AFTER 15 MINUTES BUM WENT NUMB

2

HAD 3 LARGE MUGS OF TEA. MILK, NO SUGAR IN MY HUMBLE OPINION IT IS ALMOST IMPOSSIBLE TO DRINK TOO MUCH LOVELY TEA!

3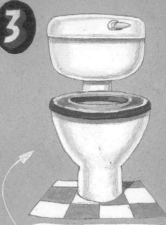

TOILET AGAIN. IT SEEMS THAT IT IS POSSIBLE TO DRINK TOO MUCH TEA

4

HAD 25 SECOND WALK AROUND THE GARDEN. (IT'S A VERY SMALL GARDEN)

5

WATCHED 'COLUMBO' ON THE BOX. HE'S A TOP-NOTCH CRIME FIGHTER AND A BIT DISHEVELLED. LIKE ME. I HAVE TO ADMIT I LIKE HIM.

6

RISKED LOOKING IN THE MIRROR. WHERE DID THAT BEARD COME FROM?

7

STARED AT SHOES FOR A BIT. THEY WERE ON THE WRONG FEET AGAIN

8

PONDERED THE UNIVERSE

9

TOOK DELIVERY OF THE PERSONALISED UNDERPANTS I ORDERED - THEY'RE JUST THE JOB

10

CALLED MOTHER SHE WASN'T IN! CALLED SISTER SHE WASN'T IN! CALLED SPEAKING CLOCK 10 PAST 2 PRECISELY!

11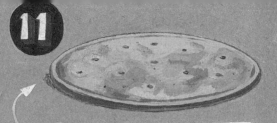

ATTEMPTED TO MAKE A HAM + CHEESE TOASTIE. COULDN'T FIND ANY HAM! ATTEMPTED TO MAKE A PLAIN CHEESE TOASTIE. COULDN'T FIND CHEESE! ATTEMPTED TO MAKE TOAST. COULDN'T FIND BREAD! HAD A BISCUIT

12

READ A COMIC ABOUT A BIONIC FOOTBALLER! —COOL!

13

SCORED THE WINNER FOR SUNDERLAND AGAINST NEWCASTLE IN THE CUP FINAL. (THE CUP FINAL THAT EXISTS IN MY HEAD)

14

SUPPED SOME POP IN BILL QUAY. FARTING TROUBLE ENSUED. NICOLA NEARLY FAINTED.

15

FOR 17½ MINUTES I DID ABSOLUTELY NOTHING. NICHT! NADA! NOWT!

16

WENT TO THE SHOP TO BUY HAM, CHEESE AND BREAD. FORGOT TO BUY HAM, CHEESE AND BREAD. REMEMBERED BUBBLEGUM

17

HAD A BISCUIT. STARED AT THE MOON. THE MOON STARED BACK AND THEN......

18

WHEN LIVING IN
A BUBBLE
HERE'S JUST A LITTLE THOUGHT
WHEN DINNERTIME ARRIVES
DON'T USE
A KNIFE AND FORK

WHY CENTIPEDES DON'T OFTEN TAP-DANCE

YES IT'S TRUE THAT MOST CENTIPEDES
DO LOVE TO DANCE
TO SALSA AND DISCO
THEY WIGGLE AND PRANCE
THEY WALTZ AND THEY FOXTROT
AND POGO TO PUNK
THEY LOVE CLASSICAL BALLET
AND JIVING TO FUNK

THEY'LL TRY ANY DANCE
FROM THE JIG TO THE TWIST
THOUGH TO TAP-DANCE
IS FAR FROM THE TOP OF THEIR LIST
WHEN YOUR LEGS COME IN HUNDREDS
INSTEAD OF IN TWO'S
IT'S JUST FAR TOO EXPENSIVE
BUYING ALL THOSE TAP SHOES!

(THE AUTHOR WOULD LIKE IT NOTED THAT ARTISTIC LICENSE HAS BEEN USED IN THESE DRAWINGS. HE COULDN'T DRAW ALL THE LEGS!)

JUNGLE ROOM

"TIDY UP YOUR ROOM YOUNG MAN!"
MAM BARKED LAST THURSDAY NIGHT
"IT'S AS MESSY AS THE JUNGLE!"
AND TO BE HONEST I THINK SHE'S RIGHT!

THERE'S A SNAKE INSIDE MY SOCK DRAW
A SLOTH INSIDE MY BED
A HOWLER MONKEY'S SWINGING AROUND
AND BOUNCING ON MY HEAD

AN OWL IS READING COMICS
THERE'S A LIZARD WHO'S WATCHING TELLY
MY HIPPO FRIEND IS TOO BIG FOR THE BATH
AND HE'S GETTING RATHER SMELLY

A PECKISH LOOKING TIGER
IS SNACKING ON MY THINGS
HE'S SWALLOWED MY ALARM CLOCK
NOW WHEN HE BURPS IT RINGS

THAT PARROT WON'T STOP TALKING
BLA-DI-BLA-DI-BLA
HE HASN'T SAID MUCH OF INTEREST YET
AND I'M NOT IMPRESSED SO FAR

THE GORILLAS ARE PLAYING FOOTBALL
WITH MY ILLUMINATED GLOBE
AND THE WINGERS HOOFED THAT FLYING WORLD
OUT THE WINDOW AND DOWN THE ROAD

ON EACH WALL, CEILING, DOOR AND FLOOR
AND EVERYWHERE ELSE THERE ARE ANTS
I'M FEELING MOST TERRIBLY ITCHY
AS THEY'RE CLIMBING RIGHT INTO MY PANTS

AND NOW I THINK I'VE HAD ENOUGH
PERHAPS MY MOTHER'S RIGHT
IT'S TIME TO TIDY UP MY ROOM
AND ENJOY A PEACEFUL NIGHT

SO "EVERYBODY OUT!" I BAWL
"IT'S TIME FOR YOU TO LEAVE"
THE HOWLER MONKEY'S HOWLING
THE HIPPO'S LOOKING PEEVED

THE SLOTH IS SLIGHTLY STIRRING
THE TIGER JUST KEEPS RINGING
THE PARROT'S CALLING ME NASTY NAMES
AND THE BIRDS HAVE ALL STOPPED SINGING

"DON'T WORRY, MY FRIENDS," I ASSURE THEM
"THERE'S REALLY NO NEED TO FEEL LOW
NEXT DOOR THERE'S ANOTHER QUITE WONDERFUL ROOM
WHERE I'M SURE THAT YOU'D ALL LOVE TO GO!"

AND SOON EVERYWHERE IS TIDY
IT'S QUIET AND SERENE
THAT IS APART FROM THE NOISE NEXT DOOR
WHERE I CAN HEAR MY SISTER'S SCREAM...

"NOW TIDY UP YOUR ROOM YOUNG LADY!"
MAM TELLS MY SISTER TONIGHT
"IT'S AS MESSY AS THE JUNGLE!"
AND TO BE HONEST I KNOW SHE'S RIGHT!

ROGER DIDN'T BELIEVE
THAT THERE WERE PEOPLE IN THE WORLD
WITH X-RAY EYES

FOR OVER AN HOUR
WE DEBATED THE MATTER
UNTIL ROGER FINALLY SAID
THAT HE COULD SEE RIGHT THROUGH MY ARGUMENT—
HE'D ALWAYS BEEN A HYPOCRITE
(AND HIS UNDERPANTS WERE HORRIBLE!)

TODAY WITH MY X-RAY EYES I SAW...

1

2

MORNING

3

....GRANDAD'S UNDERPANTS

...THE MILKMAN'S SKULL

...INSIDE CAKEBOY'S TUMMY

POOP

TODAY WHEN I STOOD IN A DOG POOP
GRAN LAUGHED LOUDLY AND SAID IT WAS LUCKY
BUT WHEN ROVER DID A POOP ON HER CARPET
SHE WENT MAD AND SAID ROVER WAS MUCKY

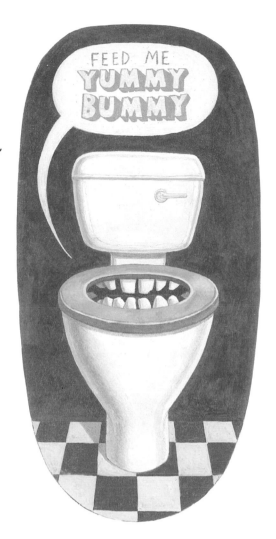

TOILET HUMOUR

GOOD JOB TOILETS DON'T HAVE TEETH
IF THEY DID THEY'D BITE YOUR BUM
YOU'D SHRIEK AND SCREAM
THEN QUICKLY JUMP OFF
LONG BEFORE THE JOB WAS DONE

PYRAMID

I'M GOING TO BUILD A PYRAMID BY THE GARDEN SHED I THINK
LIKE THE ONES FROM ANCIENT EGYPT THAT SURVIVE BESIDE THE SPHINX

I'LL FILL IT TO ITS APEX WITH THE TREASURES OF MY LIFE
THERE'LL BE TOMBS FOR BOTH MY PARENTS AND MY FUTURE STONE-DEAD WIFE

ON THE WALLS I'LL CARVE A LANGUAGE – HIEROGLYPHICS DRAWN BY ME
AND NO ONE WILL EVER DECODE IT SO ITS SECRETS WILL NEVER BE FREE

LIKE THE PHARAOHS I'LL PROBABLY NEED HELP THOUGH I'LL FLATLY REFUSE TO USE SLAVES
INSTEAD I'LL POLITELY ASK ALAN TO HELP – THAT'S A MUCH NICER WAY TO BEHAVE

ITS FAME WILL SPREAD ALL OVER OUR GLOBE AND PILGRIMS WILL TREK FROM AFAR
SO I'LL CONVERT THE OLD SHED TO A SOUVENIR SHOP OR PERHAPS A NEW SWISH CAFÉ BAR

AND WHEN ALL THE CITIES HAVE CRUMBLED, WHEN THE TREES HAVE WITHERED AND DIED
ALL YOU WILL SEE IS MY PYRAMID STANDING THERE WITH PRIDE

THEN ALIENS WILL PASS THE EARTH AND SPOT MY GREAT STRUCTURE FROM SPACE
THEY'LL ZOOM DOWN TO DISCOVER THE RICHES OF THE WORLD'S MOST SPECTACULAR PLACE

THERE'LL BE CATAPULTS, CONKERS AND BALLS, MODEL SHIPS AND REMOTE-CONTROLLED CARS
COMICS AND BOOKS AND BRIGHT GREEN FIZZY POP AND COLLECTIONS OF BUBBLEGUM CARDS

THERE'LL BE CRAYONS, PENCILS AND PAINTS, GHOST MASKS AND DINOSAUR SUITS

SHOE BOXES BRIMMING WITH WIGGLY WORMS AND GOLDFISH BOWLS SWIMMING WITH NEWTS

AND IN PRIDE OF PLACE THESE WORDS WILL BE CARVED ON A TABLET OF STONE

THAT'S BEEN BANDAGED FROM TITLE TO TOES — THE WORLD'S VERY FIRST MUMMIFIED POEM!

SO IT'S TIME TO WRAP EVERYTHING UP, TO START WORK AND TO LAY THE FIRST BRICK

YES, I'M GOING TO BUILD A PYRAMID BY THE GARDEN SHED I THINK

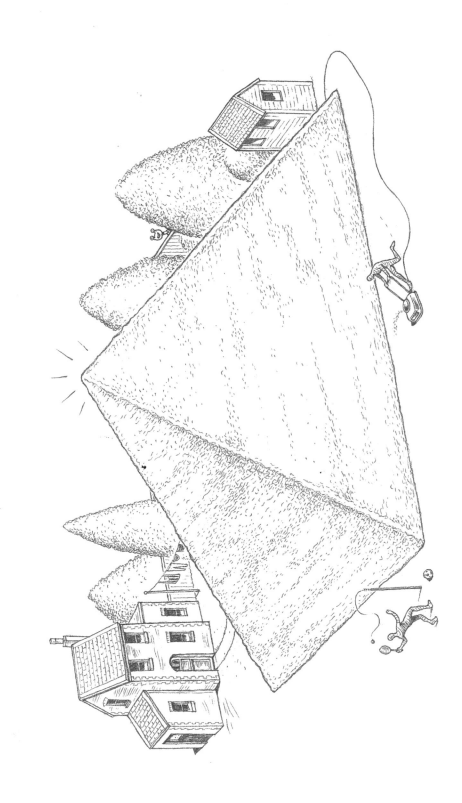

COME ON NOW TARZAN, START USING YOUR LOAF
AND STOP ALL THAT SWINGING YOU BIG MACHO OAF
SEE BEING AN APE-MAN, I JUST HAVE TO SAY
IT DON'T CUT THE MUSTARD. IT'S AWFULLY PASSÉ

IT'S THE 21ST CENTURY, MEN HAVE MOVED ON
WE'RE SENSITIVE, SOFT, OUR ROUGH EDGES HAVE GONE
YOU CAN'T GO AROUND WRESTLING LIONS AND CROCS
YOU CAN'T SLAP BIG GORILLAS THEN PELT THEM WITH ROCKS

AND AS FOR YOUNG JANE IT'S RESPECT SHE PREFERS
SO DON'T CALL HER YOUR 'CHICK' OR YOUR 'RIGHT TASTY BIRD'
IT'S JUST SO UN-P.C. AND YOU'LL END UP IN TROUBLE
UNLESS I HELP YOU GET OUT OF THIS TERRIBLE MUDDLE

THE THING TO REMEMBER IS NOT TO ACT WILD
KEEP YOUR MANNERS IN CHECK AND DELIGHTFULLY MILD
YOU SHOULD LEARN MEDITATION, LOOK AFTER YOUR SKIN
AND THOSE LEOPARD-SKIN PANTS SHOULD GO STRAIGHT IN THE BIN

THERE'S MORE...

HAVE YOUR SAUSAGES GRILLED, DON'T EAT FOOD THAT IS FRIED
GET IN TOUCH WITH THAT THING CALLED YOUR FEMININE SIDE
BUY A BOOK ON FENG SHUI AND MAKEOVER YOUR HUT
AND THEN JOIN A GOOD GYM TO AVOID A FAT GUT

HMMM, BY THE LOOK ON YOUR FACE YOU'RE NOT GREATLY IMPRESSED
IN FACT, TO BE FAIR, YOU LOOK ALMOST DEPRESSED
YOU THINK LIFE AS A NEW MAN IS JUST NOT FOR YOU
TO BE HONEST I FELT THE EXACT SAME WAY TOO

ON THE MOUNTAINS I LIVED IN THE SNOW AND THE RAIN
I WAS HAIRY, UNCOUTH, I USED BRAWN OVER BRAIN
THEN SOME HIKERS PASSED BY AND THEY TOOK ME IN HAND
AND THEY TAUGHT ME THE STUFF THAT I NOW UNDERSTAND

I CAME DOWN TO THE CITY, I CLEANED UP MY ACT
I LEARNED ETIQUETTE, MANNERS, DECORUM AND TACT
NOW FROM STAMPING AND ROARING AND LOVING TO FIGHT
FOR A MEN'S MAGAZINE ABOUT FASHION I WRITE

I AM NOW A NEW MAN, I AM CULTURED AND SUAVE
I'VE NOT BURPED OR PASSED WIND FOR A YEAR AND A HALF
'THO' I'VE JUST CHANGED MY NAME TO LORENZO SPAGHETTI
BEFORE, I WAS BEST KNOWN AS BIGFOOT THE YETI

YOU SEE, IT'S NOT REALLY AS HARD AS YOU THINK
FOR MEN TO BE CARING, TO CRY OR WEAR PINK
I IMPLORE YOU ONCE MORE, LET ME TAKE YOU AWAY
TO COACH YOU IN ALL OF THE RULES OF THE DAY

IN NO TIME THE OLD YOU WILL WOBBLE AND CRUMBLE
AT THE SIGHTS AND DELIGHTS OF YOUR NEW CONCRETE JUNGLE
JUST FOLLOW MY LEAD 'MONKEY SEE, MONKEY DO'
THERE'S NO PLACE IN THIS WORLD FOR AN APE-MAN LIKE YOU

NICE POEM, NASTY POEM?

THIS IS A POEM FULL OF SWEETNESS AND LIGHT
IT HAS PINK FLUFFY CLOUDS CRADLING LOVEBIRDS IN FLIGHT
UNDER TWINKLING STARS IT HAS LOVE AT FIRST SIGHT
AND CREAM CAKES PILED UP TO THE MOON...

OR, MAYBE...

THIS IS A POEM THAT IS RIDDLED WITH ROT
FULL OF FOUL-SMELLING WIND AND BIG STICKY GREEN SNOTS
WITH THE SCRATCHING OF BACKSIDES AND POPPING OF SPOTS
AND BURPING IN FRONT OF THE QUEEN...

HMMM?

I JUST CAN'T DECIDE HOW THIS POEM SHOULD BE
SHOULD THE WORDS BE IN SHACKLES OR ROAM AROUND FREE
I'LL SLEEP NOW AND MAYBE TOMORROW WE'LL SEE
SO 'TIL MORNING GOODNIGHT AND GOD BLESS

WHAT POEM WOULD YOU LIKE?
TICK BOX

NICE ☐   NASTY ☐

CHRISTMAS

ALL I WANT FOR CHRISTMAS IS MY TWO FRONT TEETH!
ALL I WANT FOR CHRISTMAS IS MY TWO FRONT TEETH!
ALL I WANT FOR CHRISTMAS IS MY TWO FRONT TEETH!
(OR PERHAPS A TEN-SPEED BIKE AND A COMPUTER!)

CAT'S TAIL TALE

(STARRING MONTAGUE JACK)

ON THE FIFTH OF MAY, EIGHTEEN-O-EIGHT
OLD MONTAGUE JACK SALUTED HIS FATE
WHILST SINGING SEA SHANTIES WITH A FLAGON OF ALE
THROUGH HIS TIRED RED EYES HE SPIED A CAT'S TAIL

FROM THE LEFT OF A THORN BUSH THE TAIL DID APPEAR
AS OLD MONTAGUE JACK GUZZLED BEER AFTER BEER
IT WIGGLED AND JIGGLED AND SLITHERED SO FAST
A TAIL ON ITS OWN THAT SNAKED THROUGH THE GRASS

IT PUZZLED HIM UP FROM HIS BOOTS TO HIS HAT
THERE WAS THE TAIL, BUT WHERE WAS THE CAT?
NO LITTLE PINK NOSE, TO OLD MONTY'S SURPRISE
NO WHISKERS, NO EARS, NO SHINY GREEN EYES

NO FELINE MIAOW SOUNDED AS IT DREW NEAR
BUT A STRANGE KIND OF RATTLE WAS ALL YOU COULD HEAR
AS MONTY INSPECTED THIS CURIOUS SIGHT
HE WAS SECONDS AWAY FROM A TERRIBLE FRIGHT

AS HE REACHED OUT TO STROKE THE MYSTERIOUS TAIL
HE STUMBLED AND TUMBLED AND SPILT ALL HIS ALE
THE TAIL IT WAS SOAKED BY OLD MONTAGUE'S BREW
AND IT HISSED AND IT SPAT AS ITS BAD TEMPER GREW

IT COILED **AND THEN JUMPED** AND OLD MONTY WENT NUMB
AS IT **SANK** ITS SHARP TEETH IN THE SHOCKED OLD MAN'S BUM
THEN MONTY COLLAPSED WITH A **STINGING** BACKSIDE
AND JUST **TWO** MOMENTS LATER HE CROAKED AND THEN **DIED**

THE LAST THOUGHT THAT CREPT THROUGH HIS DRUNKEN OLD BRAIN
WAS "A TAIL THAT HAS TEETH? WELL *I* **MUST BE INSANE**"
AND THROUGH DEATH'S BLACKENED DOOR HE SAW HIS MISTAKE—
THAT WILD CATLESS TAIL WAS A **BLOOMIN' BIG** SNAKE!

IF I DIE BEFORE I WAKE...

HOORAAAY!

NO
SCHOOL!!!

HAVE YOU HEARD OF THIS STUFF THEY CALL SCIENCE?

HAVE YOU HEARD OF THIS STUFF THEY CALL SCIENCE?
WHY NOT BUY SOME, UNWRAP IT THEN TRY IT?
IT WILL SHOOT YOU STRAIGHT UP TO THE MOON
CLONE A HUMAN? NOT YET, BUT QUITE SOON
IT WILL GIVE YOUR OLD GRANNY A FINE PLASTIC HIP
AND IMPRESSIVELY FLOAT A HUMUNGOUS GREAT SHIP
IT WILL BRING BACK THE HAIR TO YOUR DAD'S BALDY HEAD
CRYOGENICALLY FREEZE YOU THE MOMENT YOU'RE DEAD
BUILD A ROBOT COMPLETE WITH A HEART AND A SOUL
PREVENT BOFFINS FROM HAVING TO LIVE ON THE DOLE
TRACE A VILLAINOUS THIEF WITH HIS OWN D.N.A.
CONTACT ALIEN LIFE FROM WORLDS FAR, FAR AWAY
IT BRINGS WARMTH TO THE WINTER AND LIGHT TO THE NIGHT
IT CAN BROADEN HORIZONS AND SHARPEN THE SIGHT
SO FROM TELLY TO TOUGH GLOBAL WARMING DEFIANCE
FROM CARS TO THE AVERAGE-JOE KITCHEN APPLIANCE
AND FOR MAN AND THE EARTH'S MOST IMPORTANT ALLIANCE
IT'S LIKELY WE'LL NEED THIS GREAT STUFF THEY CALL SCIENCE
DON'T WASTE ANY TIME, CRANK YOUR BRAIN INTO GEAR
YOU COULD CHANGE WHAT YOU SEE, WHAT YOU FEEL, WHAT YOU HEAR
IF YOU USE IT CORRECTLY THERE'S NOTHING TO FEAR
BUY A BIG BOX OF SCIENCE—BRING THE FUTURE RIGHT HERE

IT WAS A SAD DAY
WHEN THE 'L' FELL OFF
THE SIGN OF THE POPULAR
LOCAL SWIMMING BATHS
YOU SEE

NO-ONE FELT QUITE THE SAME
ABOUT DIVING INTO
THE CITY MUNICIPAL POO

FAST FOOD!

EVEN FOR FAST FOOD THE KEBAB WAS QUICK
MOUTH TO TUMMY
TO BOTTOM TO TOILET!
TEN MINUTES FLAT
BEAT THAT!

MOUTH → **TUMMY** → **BOTTOM** → **TOILET**

MY TEAPOT'S FULL
OF ZEBRAS
OF CHIMPS
AND COCKATOOS
HERE'S YOUR CUP
OF CAMEL TEA
DO YOU WANT ONE HUMP
OR TWO?

MAGIC

IT'S FUN TO DELVE IN MY GRANNY'S NEW HAT
AND TO PULL OUT A RABBIT ALL FURRY AND FAT
AND FOR GRANNY TO SHRIEK "WELL, HOW DID YOU DO THAT?"
TO WHICH I REPLY "HEY, THAT'S MAGIC!!!"

IT'S TREMENDOUS TO SAW MY YOUNG COUSIN IN TWO
AS MY AUNTY CRIES LOUDLY "THIS CANNOT BE TRUE!"
SHE WEEPS AND SHE WAILS AND SHE TELLS ME SHE'LL SUE
AS I CALMLY REMARK "HEY, THAT'S MAGIC!"

IT'S A HOOT WHEN I FLOAT MY PET CAT IN THE AIR
AND MY MAM CAN'T WORK OUT HOW I GOT IT UP THERE
THE CAT IS TOO FAT AND TOO LAZY TO CARE
SO WHAT IS THE PROBLEM? IT'S MAGIC!!

IT'S A GIGGLE TO WITNESS MY BIG SISTER SOB
WHEN I TURN HER RIGHT INTO A GREEN, SLIMY FROG.
AND THEN SHE GETS CHASED BY A DIRTY GREAT DOG
I ANSWER HER CROAKS WITH "THAT'S MAGIC!"

BUT THE RABBIT HAS POOPED IN MY GRANNY'S NEW HAT
TO BE HONEST SHE'S POSITIVELY PEEVED ABOUT THAT
SHE'S SCRUNCHED UP HER BROW AND SHE'S CALLED ME A RAT
EVEN THOUGH I SAY "GRANNY, IT'S MAGIC!"

HMM, MY COUSIN'S UNFORTUNATELY STILL SPLIT IN TWO
HE'S HALF IN THE KITCHEN AND HALF IN THE LOO
AND MY AUNTY IS BAWLING, SHE CAN'T FIND THE GLUE
AS I SHEEPISHLY WHISPER "IT'S MAGIC!"

84

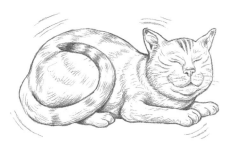

MY CAT IS STILL FLOATING. I'M READY FOR BED
BUT IT'S COUGHED UP A FUR BALL ON DAD'S BALDY HEAD
MY MOTHER'S BLIND RAGE IS NOW TURNING HER RED
AS I THINK TO MYSELF "IS THIS MAGIC?"

MY SISTER, STILL GREEN, WOULD BE HOPPITY MAD
IF SHE WASN'T SO TEARY AND, QUITE FRANKLY, SAD
AND FOR ONCE IN MY LIFE, YES, I DO FEEL QUITE BAD
BUT IT'S NOT ALL MY FAULT, IT'S JUST MAGIC!

FROM MY ROOM I CAN HEAR AS THEY SHOUT UP THE STAIR
WITH THEIR RANTING AND RAVING, IT'S BEDLAM DOWN THERE
AND THEY'RE ALL BLAMING ME WHICH IS SURELY NOT FAIR
IF SOMETHING'S TO BLAME THEN IT'S MAGIC!!

THEY'RE NOW ON THE LANDING, THEY'RE COMING FOR ME
A MORE LIVID FAMILY THERE NEVER COULD BE.
IF THEY CATCH ME I'LL POSSIBLY NEVER GET FREE
SO ONE VERY LAST TIME I NEED MAGIC.

AS I CROUCH ON THE FLOOR, THROUGH THE KEYHOLE I PEER
THEY'RE OUTSIDE THE DOOR AND I'M SHAKING WITH FEAR
NOW THEY'RE TURNING THE KNOB. OH! THE END COULD BE NEAR!
I NEED A GREAT TRICK, RIGHT NOW AND RIGHT HERE.

SO I SHOUT "ALAACAZAAM!" AND WIGGLE MY EARS
AND INTO THIN AIR I INSTANTLY... POOF!...

DISAPPEAR!

NOW I'M SURE YOU'LL AGREE, "HEY, THAT'S MAGIC!"

HILLS

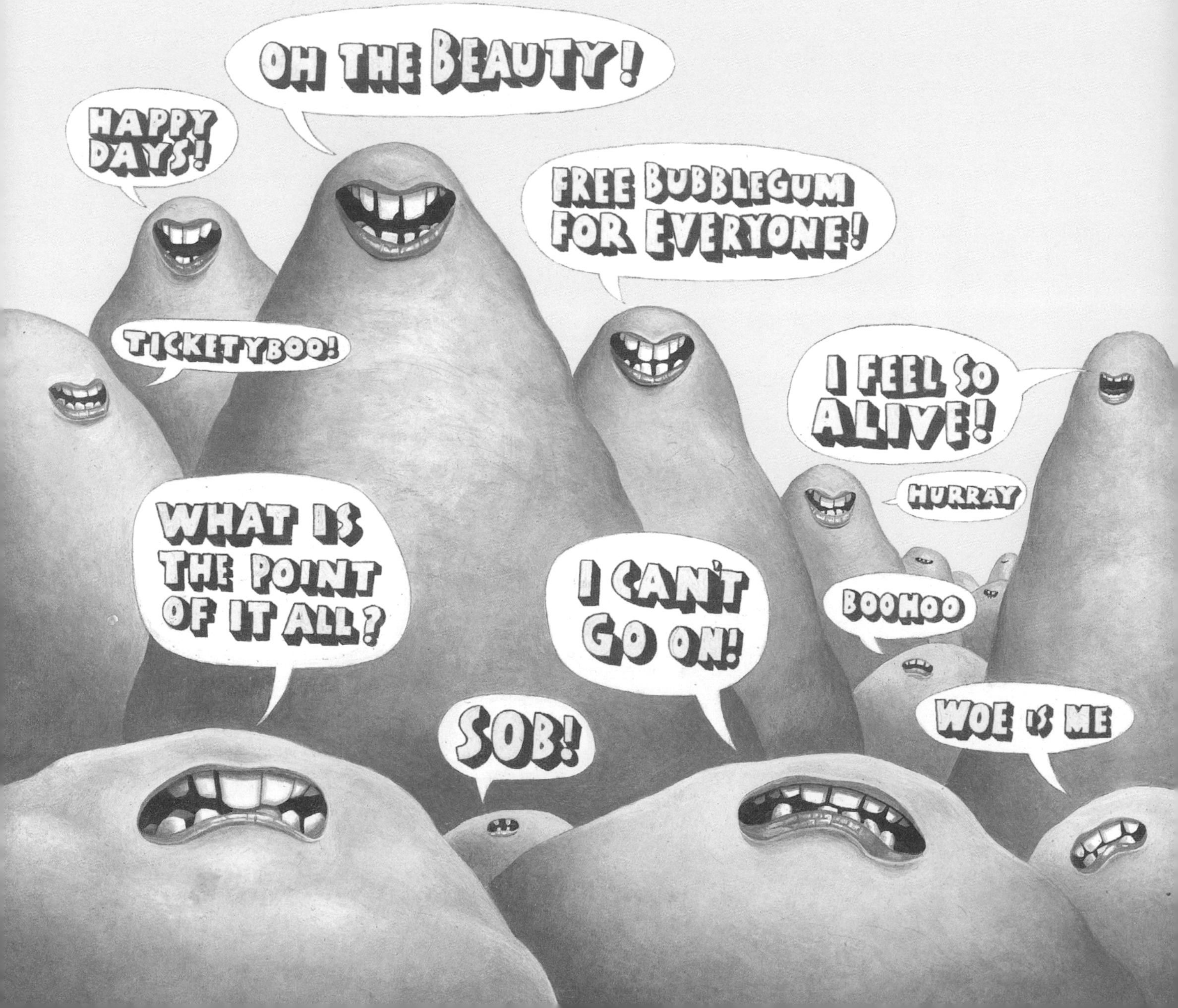
HAPPY DAYS!
OH THE BEAUTY!
FREE BUBBLEGUM FOR EVERYONE!
TICKETYBOO!
I FEEL SO ALIVE!
HURRAY
WHAT IS THE POINT OF IT ALL?
I CAN'T GO ON!
BOOHOO
SOB!
WOE IS ME

WITH THE ARRIVAL OF THE HILLS
THE LANDSCAPE BECAME PRONE
TO DRAMATIC MOOD SWINGS
UP ONE MINUTE
DOWN THE NEXT
AND NOTHING IN BETWEEN
BUT IT WAS FAR AND AWAY
BETTER THAN BEFORE
THE HILLS ARRIVED

THEN THE MOOD
HAD ALWAYS BEEN
JUST FLAT

I'M OFF TO SEE THE QUEEN
SHE'S ASKED TO SEE ME SPECIALLY
AND I HAVE TO ADMIT I'M NERVOUS
'CAUSE SHE'S RIGHT TOP PROPER ROYALTY

I'M OFF TO SEE THE QUEEN
I JUST DON'T KNOW WHAT TO WEAR
DO YOU RECKON SHE'D LIKE MY SEQUINED PANTS
OR DO YOU THINK SHE'S A BIT OF A SQUARE?

I'M OFF TO SEE THE QUEEN
ON THE WAY I'LL BUY HER A PRESENT
I'M PLANNING TO SPEND A TENNER AT LEAST
OR SHE COULD POSSIBLY THINK I'M A PEASANT

I'M OFF TO SEE THE QUEEN
I'M GOING TO TAKE ALONG MY BALL
SHE ENJOYS A GOOD PENALTY SHOOT-OUT
AND SHE ISN'T HALF TASTY IN GOAL

I'M OFF TO SEE THE QUEEN
PERHAPS WE'LL LISTEN TO SOME TUNES
HEAVY METAL IN THE MORNING
THEN PUNK ROCK IN THE AFTERNOON

I'M OFF TO SEE THE QUEEN
I HOPE SHE RUSTLES UP SOME FOOD
IF NOT I COULD TAKE ALONG SANDWICHES
OR I WONDER IF THAT WOULD BE RUDE?

I'M OFF TO SEE THE QUEEN
I REALLY SHOULDN'T WORRY
WE'LL PROBABLY SINK A COUPLE OF PINTS
THEN POP OUT FOR A CURRY

I'M OFF TO SEE THE QUEEN
IT'S TIME THAT I WAS GONE
MY BUS IS DUE IN A MINUTE OR TWO
OH I HOPE THAT NOTHING GOES WRONG

FOR THE QUEEN IS MOST IMPORTANT
TO THIS GREEN AND PLEASANT LAND
AND IT'S ME SHE'S WANTS TO SEE
SO I MUST BE A PART OF HER PLAN

YES, SHE'S BOUND TO HAVE HER REASONS
AND I HOPE THEY'RE NOT TOO SINISTER
NO, I'M SURE SHE'LL WELCOME ME WARMLY
AFTER ALL, I AM THE PRIME MINISTER

DEPRESSED
AND GLUM
OLD TYRE WAS
DEFLATED
BUT WHEN
FOOT PUMP ARRIVED
OLD TYRE WAS
ELATED

MISERY

I DON'T LIKE BROCCOLI
I DON'T LIKE BED
I DON'T LIKE HATS
AND I DON'T LIKE YOUR HEAD

I HATE GOING SWIMMING
I CAN'T STAND TO SING
I HATE DOGS THAT HOWL
AND WHEN TELEPHONES RING

I LOATHE BLACK AND WHITE
AND ALL SHADES OF PINK
AND TOILETS IN BATHROOMS
THAT STINK BY THE SINK

I'M ANNOYED AT THE RAIN
I'M AT WAR WITH THE GALES
I SHUN THE BRIGHT SUN
AND THE SNOW AND THE HAIL

I LIKE TO BE BOTTOM
I RUN FROM THE TOP
I HATE WRITING POEMS
SO I'M JUST GOING TO STOP!

93

WHAT
CAME
FIRST?

AT THE DAWN OF TIME GOD TOOK A SLURP OF TEA,
SHUFFLED IN HIS CHAIR, PICKED UP HIS PEN

AND BEGAN

"WHAT SHALL I DO FIRST?
HMMM? I'LL CREATE A CHICKEN

OR PERHAPS AN EGG

YES AN EGG!

OR MAYBE A CHICKEN

NO! AN EGG!

YES, DEFINITELY AN EGG!

THEN AGAIN A CHICKEN WOULD BE NICE

YES! CHICKEN!

THAT'S DECIDED!

ABSOLUTELY CHICKEN!

EGG, EGG, EGG, EGG, EGG, EGG,
EGGITY EGG, EGG, EGG, EGG!!!!

I'LL CREATE

AN EGG

OR PERHAPS A CHICKEN" ETC, ETC AND SO ON

THE REBEL

(THE NICEST MONSTER IN TOWN)

THERE ONCE WAS A MONSTER WHO LIVED IN OUR TOWN
HE ALWAYS SMILED BRIGHTLY AND NEVER WOULD FROWN
HE'D TIP HIS TOP HAT AND THEN SING YOU A SONG
HE'D DO EVERYTHING RIGHT, NEVER ANYTHING WRONG!

THUG WAS HIS NAME AND HE HAD A GREAT DREAM—
TO CRASH AND TO BASH AND TO SHOUT AND TO SCREAM
TO FRIGHTEN HIS FRIENDS AND HIS WHOLE NEIGHBOURHOOD
TO BE HORRIBLY BAD AND NEVER BE GOOD.

HIS WISH WAS TO WEAR THE BIG GOLDEN CROWN—
THE MARK OF THE SCARIEST MONSTER IN TOWN
FOR THE TOWNSFOLK TO SHIVER AND TREMBLE WITH FRIGHT
AS HE RAMPAGED THE STREETS FROM MORNING TILL NIGHT

FOR RESPECTABLE MONSTERS THE NAME OF THE GAME
WAS TO ALWAYS MAKE TROUBLE AND NEVER BE TAME
SO EACH DAY THEY ALL TRIED THEIR HARDEST TO BE
AS BAD AS GOOD MONSTERS COULD POSSIBLY BE

THERE'S MORE...

THEY'D PUFF OUT THEIR CHESTS AND THEY'D STAMP DOWN THEIR FEET
NEVER OFFER OLD LADIES THE VERY LAST SEAT
THEY'D CHASE FLUFFY CATS AND THEN EAT THEM WITH CHIPS
OR THEY'D MUNCH BARKING DOGS WITH TORTILLAS AND DIPS

THEY'D BURST CHILDREN'S BALLS AS THEY WOLFED DOWN THEIR TEA
THEY'D BURP IN THE LIBRARY AND WEE IN THE SEA
THEY NEVER WATCHED BALLET OR GAVE PAINTINGS A LOOK
NEVER CRIED AT THE OPERA OR READ A GOOD BOOK

THEY WERE SNOTTY AND SPOTTY WITH GREASY GREEN HAIR
AND THE SMELL OF THEIR BREATH WAS JUST TOO MUCH TO BEAR
THEY NEVER TOOK SHOWERS OR CLIPPED THEIR TOENAILS
AND THEIR BOTTOMS WERE STINKY, ESPECIALLY THE MALES

OF COURSE THIS WAS THE RIGHT WAY FOR MONSTERS TO BE
A PAIN IN THE BACKSIDE FOR YOU AND FOR ME
BUT THE TROUBLE WITH THUG, AT THE END OF THE DAY
HE WAS JUST FAR TOO PLEASANT TO END UP THAT WAY

HIS SCOWL WOULD EMERGE AS A BEAMING WHITE SMILE
THE SMELL OF HIS ARMPITS WAS FRAGRANT, NOT VILE
HIS COMPLEXION WAS FRESH AS THE PURE DRIVEN SNOW
AND MOST FACTS ABOUT SOAP HE WAS LIKELY TO KNOW

ON SUNDAY HE LOVED TO READ WORDSWORTH AND KEATS
AND HE SHARED WITH THE TOWNSFOLK HIS DOUGHNUTS AND SWEETS
HE ASSISTED FRAIL GRANNIES WHEN CROSSING THE STREET
HE CARRIED THEIR BAGS HOME THEN MASSAGED THEIR FEET

AND SOON IT WAS KNOWN THROUGHOUT ALL OF THE LAND
(A FACT THAT MOST MONSTERS COULD NOT UNDERSTAND)
THAT THUG WAS MOST GRACIOUS AND CHEERFUL AND KIND
A MORE CHARMING MONSTER YOU NEVER WOULD FIND

OTHER MONSTERS WOULD GOSSIP OVER GALLONS OF BEER
AND ONE THING YOU'D ALWAYS BE CERTAIN TO HEAR
WAS THAT THUG WAS A BLACK SHEEP, A FIEND AND DISGRACE
A BAD APPLE WHO LET DOWN THE WHOLE MONSTER RACE

IN A STRANGE KIND OF WAY THUG ACHIEVED HIS BIG GOAL
A REBEL HE WAS FROM DEEP DOWN IN HIS SOUL
BUT NOT AS A MONSTER SURROUNDED BY VICE
HE REBELLED JUST BY SMILING AND BEING SO NICE
SO...
IF YOU HEAR A STRANGE BUMP WHEN YOU'RE TUCKED UP IN BED
AND DARK THOUGHTS OF MONSTERS SUBMERGE YOU IN DREAD
THERE'S NO NEED FOR FEAR, THERE'S NO NEED FOR FLIGHT
IT'S PROBABLY JUST THUG COME TO KISS YOU GOODNIGHT!

I DON'T KNOW THE ANSWER
I'M REALLY CONFUSED
I'M HANGING MY HEAD
AS I STARE AT MY SHOES

I'M ALL OF A DITHER
I'M PUZZLED, BEFUDDLED
MY BRAIN'S SQUASHED AND MASHED
AND I'M ALL IN A MUDDLE

I'M QUITE OVERAWED
I'M OUT OF MY DEPTH
I'M IN A RIGHT PICKLE
I'M ALL OUT OF STEP

I'M SO UNENLIGHTENED
I'M DEFINITELY JADED
MY JUDGEMENT IS CLOUDY
MY REASON HAS FADED

I DON'T KNOW THE ANSWER
I CAN'T GET IT SUSSED
IT'S A BAFFLING CONUNDRUM
I'M COMPLETELY NON-PLUSSED

BUT.... WAIT!

JUST A MOMENT!
IT'S COMING TO ME
THE THICK FOG IS LIFTING
AT LAST I CAN SEE

MY COGS ARE NOW TURNING
THE PUZZLE IS CLEAR
MY BRAIN IS RELIEVED
THE ANSWER IS HERE

AND
THE
ANSWER
IS
SPROUTS
HOORAY!!!
OH
NO!

I OUGHT TO BE HAPPY
AND NOT QUITE SO MUDDLED
BUT THINGS AREN'T THAT SIMPLE
I'M STILL MOST BEFUDDLED

I'M ALL OF A DITHER
I'M REALLY CONFUSED
I'M HANGING MY HEAD
AS I STARE AT MY SHOES

YOU SEE...

FINDING THE ANSWER
IS NOT WHAT IS TESTING
THE PROBLEM IS NOW
I'VE FORGOTTEN THE QUESTION!

DON'T!

DON'T TRY CATCHING ARROWS
DON'T EVER KICK A BOMB
DON'T TRY HEADING CANNONBALLS
DON'T WRESTLE WITH KING KONG

DON'T LUNCHEON IN A DUNGEON
DON'T BOUNCE UPON A SPIKE
DON'T GO ROUND SNOGGING CROCODILES
DON'T WEAR YOUR PANTS TOO TIGHT

DON'T DARE TO FLY TOO CLOSE TO THE SUN
DON'T RUSH A VINDALOO
DON'T HUG A PRICKLY PORCUPINE
DON'T BOX A KANGAROO

DON'T SNIFF THE BUM OF A PONGY SKUNK
DON'T JUGGLE IN THE DARK
DON'T INVITE IN A VAMPIRE FOR NIBBLES AND DRINKS
DON'T PAT A PECKISH SHARK

DON'T CHOOSE TO IGNORE THIS WISE ADVICE
DON'T GAMBLE WITH YOUR HEAD
IN FACT TO BE COMPLETELY SAFE
DON'T EVER LEAVE YOUR BED!

THE SIMPLE
10-POINT GUIDE TO BRAIN-THINKING

1 THINKING IS IMPORTANT
IT HAPPENS IN YOUR HEAD
IN YOUR BRAIN TO BE MORE PRECISE. THINKING IS THE ANTIDOTE TO BEING MUDDLED
AND BEFUDDLED OR JUST PLAIN TROUBLED
IT COMES IN THE FORM OF THOUGHTS

2 THESE THOUGHTS HELP YOU TO SURVIVE MATHS TESTS
AND TO DEVISE CUNNING PLANS TO AVOID HAVING A BATH
THEY ARE THE FUEL FOR GREAT ART SUCH AS THAT MOANING LISA
GREAT LITERATURE, SUCH AS DOUGAL'S DEEP-SEA DIARY (BY SHAKESPEARE, I THINK)
AND GREAT SCIENCE, SUCH AS THE INVENTION OF THE TELLY

3 THOUGHTS CAN GROW LIKE SEEDS—FROM BABY INKLINGS INTO
HUGE CONCEPTS OR EVEN
MIGHTY VISIONS!
SUCH MIGHTY VISIONS SOMETIMES TURN UP FULLY FORMED
THIS IS CALLED A FLASH OF
INSPIRATION

PEOPLE WHO HAVE HAD THESE INCLUDE ISAAC NEUTRON (WHEN AN APPLE FELL ON HIS BONCE) AND THAT GREEK BLOKE WHO SHOUTED EUREKA! IN THE BATH IF YOU HAVE A FLASH OF INSPIRATION YOUR HEAD WILL BE CRAMMED FULL OF THOUGHTS LIKE SARDINES IN A TIN YOU WILL NOT BE ABLE TO SLEEP

4 FLASHES OF INSPIRATION CAN OCCUR AT ANY TIME ON TELLY THEY HAPPEN WHEN PEOPLE ARE STANDING ON MOUNTAINS OR STARING AT SUNSETS IN REAL LIFE THEY ARE MORE LIKELY TO ARRIVE WHEN YOU ARE WHISTLING ON THE TOILET OR PICKING YOUR NOSE ON THE BUS

5 SOMETIMES THE LIGHT WILL BE ON BUT THERE'LL BE NO-ONE AT HOME THIS MEANS YOUR THINKING IS HAZY OR LAZY OR EVEN NON-EXISTENT YOU MAY BE CALLED A DOOLEY OR A DUNCE OR A PLANK ONCE MY THINKING WAS SO LAZY AND HAZY I ENDED UP WITH MY HEAD STUCK IN A BUCKET...

GUESS WHAT...?

6 ...IF YOU GET YOUR HEAD STUCK IN A BUCKET
YOU WILL NEED TO CONCENTRATE
CONCENTRATION IS HOW YOU GLUE TOGETHER MANY THOUGHTS
TO HELP YOU SOLVE A PROBLEM
PROBLEMS CAN ALSO BE SOLVED WITH BRAIN FOOD
MAM SAYS THAT SPROUTS ARE BRAIN FOOD AND THEY HELP YOU TO THINK
THAT'S WRONG. FUDGE SUNDAES AND CHIPS HELP ME TO THINK!

7 SOMETIMES IT'S IMPORTANT TO THINK BEFORE YOU SPEAK. THIS STOPS YOU FROM
PUTTING YOUR FOOT IN IT
ONCE I DIDN'T THINK BEFORE I TOLD GRANNY SHE HAD TUNA-CAT-BREATH
THIS WAS A MISTAKE
SHE DIDN'T VISIT FOR TWO MONTHS AND MAM GOT UPSET
(BUT AT LEAST GRANNY STARTED TO SUCK MINTS)

8 IF YOU DO PUT YOUR FOOT IN IT YOU WILL NEED TO RECHARGE YOUR BRAIN LIKE A BATTERY
TO DO THIS YOU SHOULD EAT FIVE FUDGE SUNDAES AND A BUCKET OF CHIPS
THIS SHOULD NOT FAIL, BUT IF IT DOES
THEN YOU SHOULD TAKE THE MOST DRASTIC ACTION—
YOU SHOULD SLEEP ON IT
HOWEVER THIS IS COMPLICATED
WHEN YOU SLEEP STRANGE ROGUE THOUGHTS INVADE YOUR BRAIN
THESE ARE KNOWN AS DREAMS

YOU MAY DREAM THAT YOU ARE A 200-FOOT MOUSE IN A SUIT OF ARMOUR

OR A FLYING CHEESECAKE

THE MEANING OF SUCH DREAMS IS TOO DIFFICULT TO EXPLAIN HERE AND WOULD TAKE OVER AN HOUR

SO I'M NOT GOING TO BOTHER

9 ALWAYS REMEMBER YOU HAVE ONLY ONE BRAIN

SO LOOK AFTER IT

KEEP IT WARM BY WEARING A HAT (WOOLLY IF POSSIBLE BUT NO TOP HATS)

EXERCISE IT EVERY DAY

THIS IS DONE BY THINKING ABOUT SCIENCE OR RECITING THE
ALPHABET BACKWARDS, IN A SCOTTISH ACCENT AT GREAT SPEED
IF YOU NEGLECT YOUR BRAIN THEN IT MAY CONK OUT—FOR GOOD
THEN THE ONLY HOPE WOULD BE A BRAIN TRANSPLANT
HOWEVER THESE ARE EXPENSIVE AND A LITTLE TRICKY TO DO

ALL IN ALL BEST AVOIDED

BUT IF YOU TAKE CARE OF YOUR BRAIN
THEN YOUR BRAIN WILL TAKE CARE OF YOU

OUI!

NON!

10 FINALLY, TO SUM UP WHEN THINKING ABOUT THINKING ABOUT THINKING

THINK ONLY THIS

TAKE TIME TO THINK ABOUT IT AS ULTIMATELY, TO MY THINKING THINKING
ABOUT THINKING IS THE ONLY WAY TO POSSIBLY THINK ABOUT THINKING
AND THAT MUCH IS CLEAR... **I THINK!**

DON'T COOL AN APPLE PIE ON A WINDOW LEDGE
IT WILL GET STOLEN
DON'T CARRY A PANE OF GLASS ACROSS A STREET
IT WILL GET BROKEN

NEVER INVESTIGATE A CRASH IN THE CELLAR
OF A LARGE OLD HOUSE AT MIDNIGHT
YOU WILL BE EATEN
AND DON'T LEAVE YOUR ROCKET
FOR A DARING SPACEWALK
YOU WILL BE STRANDED

ALWAYS CHEER FOR THE WEEDY TEAM OF UNDERDOGS
THEY WILL WIN
AND WHEN BEING CHASED BY OVERTIRED ZOMBIES
ALWAYS TAKE THE BUS
YOUR CAR WON'T START

THINGS
I'VE
LEARNED
FROM
FILMS

NEVER WORRY ABOUT WHAT'S CASTING
A STRANGE SHADOW ON YOUR BEDROOM WALL
IT'S JUST A TREE
AND NEVER TRUST THE MAYOR OF A SMALL ISLAND TOWN—
THERE ARE SHARKS IN THE WATER
(OF COURSE THERE ARE SHARKS
THE WATER IS FULL OF SHARKS)

AND IF YOU'RE A COWBOY
GET TO KNOW THE INDIANS — AND VICE VERSA
BOTH SIDES ARE ALL RIGHT REALLY
WHEN ON A DESERT ISLAND
IMMEDIATELY GIVE UP ON BEING RESCUED
HELP WILL COME QUICKER

OBVIOUSLY DON'T TRUST THE NEW KID AT SCHOOL
HE'S PROBABLY A ROBOT
OR AT LEAST AN ALIEN

AND WHEN SITTING ALONE QUIETLY READING A BOOK OF POETRY
ALWAYS
LOOK OVER YOUR LEFT SHOULDER
THERE WILL BE A MONSTER BEHIND YOU!

I KNOW AN UNSUNG HERO
HE'S HANDSOME,
CARING AND KIND
BUT LET'S NOT DWELL
ON HIS GOOD POINTS
INSTEAD LET'S DWELL
ON MINE!

THERE IS NO DEFENCE OF THE SPROUT

OF THE SPROUT

SEND HIM DOWN

POEM IS A THIS BROKEN

COME IT'S THE TO TIME ITS OF END

FROM HEIGHT A DROPPED VERY I GREAT IT

RHYME NOW DOESN'T IT SO !